NOV 1 3 2006

ELK GROVE VILLAGE PUBLIC LIBRARY

3 125

2017 ✓

W9-APS-291

Discarded By Elk Grove
Village Public Library

ELK GROVE VILLAGE PUBLIC LIBRARY
1001 WELLINGTON AVE
ELK GROVE VILLAGE, IL 60007
(847) 439-0447

Rookie
biographies®

Theodore Roosevelt

By Wil Mara

Reading Consultant
Cecilia Minden-Cupp, PhD
Former Director of the Language and Literacy Program
Harvard Graduate School of Education
Cambridge, Massachusetts

Children's Press®
A Division of Scholastic Inc.
New York   Toronto   London   Auckland   Sydney
Mexico City   New Delhi   Hong Kong
Danbury, Connecticut

Designer: Herman Adler Design
Photo Researcher: Caroline Anderson
The photo on the cover shows Theodore Roosevelt.

Library of Congress Cataloging-in-Publication Data

Mara, Wil.
 Theodore Roosevelt / by Wil Mara.
   p. cm. — (Rookie biographies)
 Includes index.
 ISBN-10: 0-516-29844-5 (lib. bdg.)   0-516-27304-3 (pbk.)
 ISBN-13: 978-0-516-29844-3 (lib. bdg.)   978-0-516-27304-4 (pbk.)
 1. Roosevelt, Theodore, 1858–1919—Juvenile literature. 2. Presidents—United
States—Biography—Juvenile literature. I. Title. II. Rookie biography.
 E757.M358 2006
 973.91'1092—dc22   2005030087

© 2007 by Scholastic Inc.
All rights reserved. Published simultaneously in Canada.
Printed in Mexico.

CHILDREN'S PRESS, and ROOKIE BIOGRAPHIES®, and associated
logos are trademarks and/or registered trademarks of Scholastic Library
Publishing. SCHOLASTIC and associated logos are trademarks and/or
registered trademarks of Scholastic Inc.
1 2 3 4 5 6 7 8 9 10 R 16 15 14 13 12 11 10 09 08 07

Can you change the world with energy and hard work? Theodore Roosevelt did! Roosevelt was the twenty-sixth president of the United States.

Young Roosevelt

Roosevelt was born on October 27, 1858, in New York City. He had three brothers and sisters. Many people called him Teddy.

Roosevelt's parents taught their son the importance of hard work. They were very caring.

Young Roosevelt suffered from asthma (AZ-muh) and bad eyesight. He didn't let these problems stop him from working hard and learning new things.

Roosevelt grew up to be a strong and active man.

Theodore Roosevelt (back row, left) with (right to left)
his brother Elliot, sister Corinne, and family friend Edith
Kermit Carow

Roosevelt with Edith Kermit Carow and their family in 1903

Roosevelt married Alice Hathaway Lee in 1880. They had one daughter, whom they also named Alice.

Roosevelt's wife died in 1886. He later married Edith Kermit Carow. They had five children together.

Roosevelt was a good student. He went to college at Harvard University in Cambridge, Massachusetts.

Roosevelt became a politician in New York in 1882. A politician is a government official who helps to run a town, state, or country. Roosevelt held many different political jobs.

Roosevelt as the director of the New York Police Department in the mid-1890s

Roosevelt as a soldier

12

Roosevelt took a break from politics in 1898. He traveled to Cuba as a soldier in the Spanish-American War. This was a war fought between Spain and the United States that year. Roosevelt was a brave leader and a popular hero during this war.

Roosevelt returned to politics after the Spanish-American War ended.

William McKinley was elected president of the United States in 1900. Roosevelt served as McKinley's vice president.

William McKinley (left) and Roosevelt

President Roosevelt giving a speech in 1903

16

President McKinley was shot and killed on September 14, 1901. Roosevelt took over as president of the United States.

Roosevelt was only forty-two years old. He became the youngest president in American history.

American businesses were growing fast in the early 1900s. President Roosevelt made sure workers received good pay and were treated fairly.

Roosevelt (center) with workers at a steel factory in Minneapolis,
Minnesota, during the early 1900s

Roosevelt in Yosemite National Park in 1903

Roosevelt created many laws to protect nature. Some laws made sure certain forests would never be destroyed. Other laws stopped people from harming rare plants and animals.

Roosevelt arranged for the building of the Panama Canal in Central America in 1904. A canal is a waterway that is dug across land.

The Panama Canal allows ships to travel more easily between the Atlantic and Pacific oceans.

Roosevelt (center) inspecting construction of the Panama Canal in 1906

Roosevelt (center) in Portsmouth, New Hampshire, with leaders from Japan and Russia in 1905

There was a war between Russia and Japan (1904–1905) during Roosevelt's presidency.

Roosevelt won the Nobel Peace Prize for helping the leaders of Russia and Japan agree to end this conflict. The Nobel Peace Prize is one of the greatest honors in the world.

Roosevelt left the presidency in 1908. He then explored jungles in Africa and South America.

Roosevelt wrote several books about his adventures.

Roosevelt and his son Kermit (left) during a hunting trip to Africa

Copyright 1902
by M.P. RICE WASH. D.C.

28

Roosevelt died on January 6, 1919. He was sixty-one years old.

Roosevelt once said, "No man has led a happier life than I have led." He will always be remembered for his amazing energy, great leadership, and love for his country.

Words You Know

Africa

Edith Kermit Carow

Panama Canal

soldier

Theodore Roosevelt

William McKinley

Index

About the Author

Wil Mara is the author of more than seventy-five books. He has written fiction and nonfiction for both children and adults.

Photo Credits

Photographs © 2007: Corbis Images: 3 (Bettmann), 19 (Minnesota Historical Society), 12, 24, 31 top (Underwood & Underwood), cover (Oscar White), 8, 30 top right; Library of Congress: 16, 28, 31 bottom left; Theodore Roosevelt Collection, Harvard College Library: 4, 7, 11, 15, 20, 23, 27, 30 bottom, 30 top left, 31 bottom right.